The need to survive, the deep search for love, the endless waves of compassion that drive us along our different paths, convinced of our different ideas of what is worth living for.

Table of Contents

THE START

The start

'Start today,' he said, 'write for 15 minutes, not more.
Write the first chapter tonight.' 'Can I?' a child
asked.
'Yes, you can. You have to tell yourself that you can.'
'Really?'
His soft eyes spoke: 'yes.'
I fear memories will escape like lost dreams. I hold
tight a hammer to nail the starting point, knot the
rope then begin to slide, stretching out a longing as
big as a summer cloud, as misty as an English
morning, as strong as my desire to fly.
I fear pain.
I fear courage.
I fear the findings.
I fear the joy of being free.

The first paragraph

A long working day, stretched to its limits, what was
awaiting was not clear. Is it the shadow of turbulent
waves or just some scattered notes?
Is it the sewing of patchwork?
Nothing is clear yet.

The ghost

He was buried deep, disintegrating in the earth. His memory came to me in pieces, not all at once. He was there in those tiny atomic cells of my being, extending as an ocean wave in a stormy night, tipping my happy life into hell. He was there weak, invisible to everyone but shining with piercing pain in my inner face, blinding me till I swayed away from my path, then he would go for enough time for me to get up from the wreckage.

The mirror

I stood staring at the mirror. I glance at her, the version of me that shines through the bursting sun. A necklace resting made of pearls from the holy land. A silver ring worn over the mark of a gold one in an attempt to stop agony leaking out. Under my blouse hides a Syrian gold chain carrying a golden heart. Syria, in my heart, in my mind, in my thoughts and in my tears.

I looked again,
- Hey, you! It is going to be OK.

The light

And there it was, the moment between dark and light, that miracle before the birth, the birth of a new beginning, bursting into light or into a mist, and sometimes into a radiance, too much for the retina to catch.

The fear of darkness and the celebration of light I knew about before, but it was between the darkness and the birth of light that I became a witness. From that moment I followed the light, and it followed me, found me, lightened my day, or turned its back on me and dried out my smile.

It brings to my mind my country, Syria. To breathe freely and break the darkness of fear, to reach the light lies in that middle space, in that misty view through travails, in that pause where we are awaiting the birth.

THE LONG TIME AGO...

I was Born

I was born on the 27ᵗʰ of October to a mother whose name was Georgette, whose parents emigrated to Haiti. She was 23 years old when they came back. So, my mum came to Damascus while all her siblings were scattered around the world. She was the middle child; she was mild tempered. Never caused trouble, and was close to her mum, or rather her mum was close to her as she felt responsible for her daughter's unhappiness.

Yes, I was born on the 27ᵗʰ of October to a mother who 2 years prior to my arrival lost a toddler to Diphtheria. That year there was an epidemic in the country, but who cares about facts, the emotions were high. According to my dad, she killed his son by neglect. At the time, mum went back to her parents with her child. She wanted a divorce. The custom set that a woman moves from her parents' house to her husband's house then to the grave. That was the holy, bloody order. Who could say NO! Divorce was the biggest sin of all for the Christian community. So, she went back to him, abstaining from loving him; the son of a well-known family; my dad.

Yes, I was born after my parents lost their first precious child. I was born to a father in grief and a mother who was living in hell and guilt.

So, *I was born on 27th October* the year Syria lived a very short period of democracy. The Jewish midwife delivered me to this world. From the 27 of October, I lived for the first 20 years of my life in a traditional house in the Christian quarter, in the heart of the old Damascus and between its old gates.

MUM

Mum

'Her voice in Arabic was so low while in Creole it was music.'

The flower

My mother's flower was lily, a mercury element. She was made not to be crushed. Her presence is a gentle radiance. She found within herself a breathing space to be content. Her voice was music to my ears when she spoke Creole with her oldest sister Violet.

The conversation started always with:
'mari mwen pa la'
' Which means: my husband is not here.
My aunt would reply:
'IDYOT LA',' which means: 'the idiot!'

The Warmth

If I got home late and upset, I would wake her up whispering:
'Mum, give me your warm space," she moved, turned towards me half asleep and put her arms around me. Then I felt OK.

The Beauty

Humming Waltz music, she holds me gently in strong arms. I swing around looking at the sky and the tree's branches above. At the André Rieu concert, I cried for her, I closed my eyes and danced with my mum, this time there was music.
How can you appreciate beauty and be deprived from it?
How painful when dance lives within your being and music sings in your head in a deaf and deserted world?

The Strength

In no time after we'd grown up, she decided to learn to read and write in Arabic. She was so proud to sign her French letters in Arabic. It was the beginning; she went on to do more and to support the community she lived in.

Christmas

The fresh smell of coffee from the kitchen and the heat from the fire woke me up. My mother was at the bedroom door with her smiling face "Joyeux Noël mes enfants." One of her French phrases.

Dressing in our new clothes was a ceremony. The materials were bought from the best shop in town and two fittings at least at Rose's, the dressmaker. Mum helped us to put on the clothes then stood back, looking at us with such love, and exclaimed: 'You look beautiful!'.

Well, I always felt good and beautiful when I looked into my mother's eyes.

Lunch time was special, all of us sat at the table, dressed beautifully, having Christmas lunch, and listening to my father's news about his parish. My mother would nod her head to show her support for my dad's views about the bishop while her eyes moved around to be sure that we needed nothing. It didn't matter to me if my father liked the bishop or his sermon. We were sitting, eating, and listening to my dad who 'knew everything'.

This is Christmas as I remember as an eight-year-old; a warm, pleasant time, new clothes, delicious food, lots of sweets, the church bells ringing and the lovely baby Jesus.

As I grew older Christmas also grew older and sadder. Refugees fled, war erupted, there was always a reminder that there is pain nearby. All the same my mother kept making Christmas special.

Easter celebration

The silence falls for a moment. Mum rests the velvet dress on the bed and the new shoes with the white socks tucked in next to the bed. I rest my hand on the dress, caress it, run my hand along the dress, velvet...

The skin of my newborn, the delicate fresh skin cushioned with her barely heard pulse, velvet, like velvet.
The rose perfume evaporating as the petals drop. I pick one, velvet, like velvet.
The cream caramel spoonful sliding through my throat, velvet, like velvet.

I touched the velvet of my dress that day; I touched promises...
of celebrations
of happy moments,
of longing and reaching,
of hugging and melting,
of endless ripples
of renewed moments of moments
of surrender, surrender to let the cells breath,

12

let the body dissolve into the moment,
into the place ...
into velvet...
velvet...

DAD

Dad

I feared his loud voice but felt his gentleness reading poetry,
When he welcomed to his Parish all humankind,
his sensitivity when I sat next to him, watching the first play,
listening to the first concert.

Mariam,

the once a week cleaner, mum's helper

Mariam claimed she could read coffee cups, so while dad turned his coffee cup upside down, she would call us to the kitchen and ask us about his news.

'She is good, isn't she?'

It was hilarious to watch dad's astonished face. If we were late from school or left early after lunch, she had to make up stories.

'She is talking rubbish!' Dad concluded after a while.

The temple

In the holy temple sat my dad
I knocked quietly
'Come in', dad would say,
I would enter,
collect words that had fallen from the bookshelves,
a kiss, a hug I had missed
in the rush of the day before,
a stern look through his glasses and his smoke.
He's been gone for too long to remember
The temple has vanished and so has God's mercy.
I've sobbed since, and so has the earth.

The library

At his gigantic desk he sat, resting his hands on the leather pad, books open wide, spread out with the daily paper. It was the only part of his office I could see as I stood in the yard looking in through the door that stood open a crack.

'Dad?' I would call. With one hand he would push the cigarette smoke aside, his beard tarnished by the nicotine, then remove his glasses and he would say 'Come,' with a loving voice

I stepped into that kingdom. shelves set into the wall with wooden shutters bursting with books. The jewel was the glass cabinet, beautifully made.

We were told that his books are for 'grown-ups'; an open invitation to raid that library!

My sister and I slip in. She is two years younger. She grabs any two books and I make sure there is no sign of our intrusion.

In the first raid, my sister got 'War and Peace. It took her ages to finish it, while I got hold of a Guy de Maupassant novel. Mine took less time to read but a longer time crying my eyes out, concluding after two more tragic novels that men are bastards!

If he left for the day, then we ran in. One of us would get hold of the biggest book and pretend to read like him, and the other, usually me, would attempt to sit in his chair and reach his desk.

One of my fondest memories is being invited to a demonstration called:

'How to use a fountain pen, how to fill it with ink and how to dry the nib'

That took place at his desk. That day I felt crowned with pride.

The loved one

The Christening

The boy was called Habib, the loved one, who arrived to heal my dad's pain for the loss of my older brother, Saad. The Christening of my brother Habib is the most framed memory of my life.

Leading up to the christening and the celebration, the house was full of so many well-wishers who stepped in to help. It was a community celebration for a boy that would bring love back to our home. Long tables with white linen, the dishes were a beautiful tapestry exploding with colours, surrounded by the lemon tree blossoming with flowers. The water fountain ran quietly in the courtyard and the aroma of jasmine spread with every breeze that passed by. Everyone was happy, including my parents.

Cheers! To the loved one! To health!
They raised their glasses again and again.

The Protection

The priest lifts up the baby. Everyone crosses
themselves.
The priest plunges the baby in the water and lifts him
again.
The baby screams and people smile. *He is baptised.*
A pure cotton shawl wraps the baby and soft hands
hug him to rest,
piercing pain with holy joy.

I wish

The siren wailed.

'Where is your brother?'

I ran upstairs to reach the terrace, my little brother stood there under the vine leaves, unaware. At the last step I saw a plane far away, dropping its bombs, one, two, three... I froze in my place. I screamed his name. He survived then but life kept chasing him. Thoughts kept fighting in his strong-built body and soft delicate brain His green eyes seemed clouded sometimes and as clear as a calm sea at others.

He touched my head once, gently, smiled and said:

'Sister, you are saved, I was not'

'No, don't say that little brother'

I held him. I wish I was God. I wish I was magic. I only managed to buy him a perfume he would like.

The Castle

There are two gates to reach the outside world. The main gate is a small door with a giant door knocker - a cannon that sneezes from time to time. The second gate is a magic crossing from our terrace to the neighbour's, done skilfully with little feet.

In a courtyard paved with patterned tiles, a silver lake is trapped in a stone cage. A fountain that sprays water and lanterns of laughter. The citrus tree's blossom promises yellow fruits giggling between the leaves. Sun shines through it and leaves warm shadows with spots of light that dance in the symphony of leaves.

A wandering vine slides upwards, smooth as a stream, to the terrace where four posts stand linked by a canopy of strings, all in preparation for the vine-woman to rest, naked in winter without shame and so full in late summer with juicy grapes which explode with joy at the touch of a lip.

Those beautiful chandeliers are far from our reach. The juicy sun brushed grapes are hard to resist. My father's warnings about 'the danger of falling from the terrace edge' do not stop us. We have the youthful urge to grip the now. There is no thought of tomorrow.

On the other wall a jasmine bush drapes itself around the salon window, half asleep and half dreaming of voices. A tortoise treads with steady, cautious steps. Another corridor leads to the kitchen and a storage room hidden where quiet curses were whispered freely, in the shade and out of hearing.

There in the dark storage room, between the jars of jam and pickles, are many neglected things left from a century before. Things gathered by generations against a later time of drought.

There lived the four of us with mum and dad.

The Hidden room

IF WE CHOOSE, WE CAN LIVE LIFE A WORLD OF
COMFORTING ILLUSION

In a room as big as the school yard,
as haunted as the frightened soul,
as high as the path to God,
as bright as the Rattle of a cattle
in a field so far away,
As dark as the secret of a stained mind,
As deep as my mother's hold

There lived a goat and a few sheep that grazed from
the green field shadowed by trees. Filling their thirst
from a stream all set in paintings hanging on a wall
I shook my delicate wings and disappeared in the
hidden room.
There I sat at the feet of the big chair watching the
sheep sipping water and eating grass, wondering what
would happen if the water stopped flowing and the
grass was all eaten and the trees lost their leaves.
What would happen to these sheep? Would the picture
become bare? Should we bury them in the family
cemetery? I fell more than once from the painting,
half asleep and dreaming of ways to get more grass.
From time to time, I still wash my face with rose

27

water, set the scene on the wall and jump in to watch the dream.

Next door

Our home was in a neighbourhood made by the gathering of different religions rather than a class. As communities leant on each other so houses were also tangled and held tight to each other. The poor families' houses filled the gaps between the rich spacious houses. They too had their state and presence. From the terrace and through the thin walls that separated us we heard the neighbours, the laughter, and the arguments.

In that tiny house, there was only one big room, like magic, the floor of mattresses and the smell of sleep turned into a fresh, bright sitting room during the day. As for their tiny kitchen, it held enough space to prepare their daily food. Storage was not needed as their food relied on their daily income. Even the sun had to crowd itself into their little yard, but it managed to fit there and dry their hand washed clothes. A few rays were left to nurture an aromatic jasmine plant that breathed scent in the late afternoon.

We reached them by crossing from our terrace to theirs. We busied ourselves watching the neighbours as we gathered the washed linen that stored the sun in its fibres. I am too like that linen; I need a breath of fresh air and a sun ray to penetrate my being to function well.

The Alley

I open the door and follow my feet,
Um Riyad is opening windows,
brushing away last night's sleep,
Um George is sweeping outside her door,
Um Abdo shouting in the lane,
Um Nawal calling her husband

I go through that alley again,
and it turns into a fun fair.
We run red faced, gasping for breath like cute little
mice,
While our mothers finish their chats

I go through that alley again, touching the walls.
On the first wall, rest overgrown Jasmine branches.
The second wall is scratched
where a car couldn't squeeze
into the miniature street.
The third wall is smooth to touch.
The fourth wall needs repairs
but the father is ill there,
nobody's to blame.

I go again walking that alley looking for those passing through.
School uniforms rush through, a bicycle brushes us.
We jump in fear, curse him, and laugh.
I walk as though blind, hearing, touching then crying from joy.
I lived there once.

The Sounds of my vision

A step in the lane is a sign of danger.
A cry at midnight is a place not to approach.
A shout from over the fence: someone's been beaten.
A giggle, and I know the fountain is working
the church bell rings joyful at midnight,
 a child has just been born.
The bell's slow echo, a funeral approaching.
The piercing shout of cars' horns,
The bride is about to arrive.
The doorbell rings.
Who is that?
I run and hide.

My people

The schoolmistress

The school bell rings. It irritates our warm skin and our body of sweat. We run and stand in line waiting for her piercing voice:

- MOVE!

34

On the stairs, our feet tapping, our heads spinning, our body engine roaring. Her words descend like thunder:

- WHO IS TALKING?

By the time we got to the class, we were little worms. sitting like sardines in a tin, yet we shell out the fear; the giggle starts again.

I look at the tall window, we will be out, out of her reach soon. Her monster piercing voice will eat her up!

The history teacher

In years 7, 8, and 9, my daydreaming ballooned in history lessons. I had no other choice but to listen to her quivering voice. Let me describe her; a bare face, two black line eyebrows, two red spot cheeks, uttering war history from two thin lips sniffing with a rabbit's nose buttered with Nivia.

I step out of the place, climbing the mountain away
from war then slide towards the fields.

I collect some lemons from our tree, then jump from
one house to another like our cat till I reach the field
of forbidden things. I kiss my dad's friend's son and
we look at each other. I count every cell on his
cheeks, I count every wink from his beautiful eyes
framed by his thick glasses.

- *The bell is ringing; my friend nudges me.*

We fly the stairs as dancing wasps. Run out to the
street, as starving ants. I wash my hands. Eat fast.
Run out to join the race, till we are out of breath.

Back to the school, the teacher is in the capsule of my
sight, but I am in the fields of dreams, finishing what
I missed.

The Maths Teacher

I drew 3 lines with the white chalk on the blackboard.

- Straight, straight, a straight line carries one truth...

My line goes up, my line goes down, sometimes.
it goes in a circle that goes round and round
and round in a maze.

My fingers get hold of a line,
it is halo above my head.
then, slips, a hula hoop around my waist,
slides as a cylinder, wrapping my body.

- stand in the corner, you broke the line!

My back to the blackboard and the dust of the chalk
My back to the harshness of adult rules.
I see the yard with the blossoming tree.
I can't wait to slide on a strand of light.

The child of a broken straight line is me.

Samira

Samira told as many girls as she could:
'Because you are my friend, I am going to tell you a secret, but please don't tell anyone. Samir is my boyfriend!'

She wanted to make sure no one would respond to his flirting or fancy him. The whole school knew by the time he found out. She acted with shock and pretended to cry then revealed in an innocent voice:
'The only one I told is the priest's daughter!'

It did not matter that she lied. That was the most childish of secrets and lies after all.
After we finished year 9 and the general exam, she did not come back to school. After her parents learned about Samir, the first suitor who came along became her husband. Then she learned that her oldest sister who worked abroad and had always been so kind was her mum, and those horrible old parents were her grandparents.

I saw her a few years later holding a toddler by one hand and pushing the buggy with a baby in with the

other. I recognised her from the way she moved her hair and her head.

'You have not changed,' she said.

'You have lovely children,' I said.

We added a few more sentences to close the awkwardness of the unplanned encounter.

'Bye'

'Bye'

I walked away a few steps then stopped to look back at her. She did the same too. So, I turned back to where she stood waiting for me. By the time I reached her I had reached back to the classroom of our school. We embraced the giggles and the small dreams that never went further than our school gate. We passed the time of innocence. She held her toddler's hand ready to cross the road and I headed towards the bus stop. Under the dark blanket of the night, we disappeared to one another.

'I was rushing as you do when you're 19 and the world is waiting for you. In a hurry you see figures moving rather than people with features"

Ghada

'You live in a room!'
'Yes, in a room, but in a very big house'
I carried the question again to my mum.

'How come?'
'Well, my child, not everyone has money, her dad
does not earn enough money'
'But mum, Ghada is always smiling.'
'That is very good, she is happy because she lives in a
happy family and that matters a lot, my child, a lot.'

Nobody at home told me that others are lesser than
us.
It was the opposite; it was the bloody opposite!

'Look at these peasants near the lamp post. They don't
have electricity and after school they help their
parents in the field, still they do their study at night
under the streetlamp on the main road'
'Look, in my parish some live in one bedroom. These
children will become doctors and engineers'
When it comes to food, the talk was about people
starving in Africa.

I did not become a doctor, but I managed to read and write and pass my exams, despite daydreaming out of boredom.

The others

The Greek Orthodox church school, the same school my dad attended, was five minutes' walk, or over twenty minutes if you take the indirect way passing near friend's houses.

At school, there was a group of children who never looked happy. At the end of a school day when we burst out running wildly, this group of children used to stand in rows of two till all of them were there. They did not wear our uniform, they wore theirs; dark coloured clothes, and walked rigidly till they disappeared.

'Why?' I carried the question to mum,
'They are orphans, they don't have parents.'
'Who looks after them?'
'The nuns'

'They are so unhappy, mum!'

Mum reached out and hugged me and there was
silence.
There was a lot of silence in our house even with four
unruly kids full of life, even with the endless
discussions with dad about anything, there was
silence, inner silence, I don't know why. I carried it
for years to come. My sorrow lives in that silence, and
my aching and my longing live there, too.

Elias

I saw our old next-door neighbour leaving his house one morning. I watched him from an upstairs window. He turned the corner then disappeared. In a day or two, I heard my parents saying that he'd died. I concluded that death is when we go on a journey and never come back. We lined up next to the Cathedral, the endless funeral ceremonies weighted equally with the car horns of so many weddings and christenings. It made sense for a child to think; 'this is the cycle of life!'

The first-time death disturbed me was when a neighbour's oldest son died in a fire making candles for the church. His death was caused by his own efforts to put the fire out, fearing his dad would be angry, while his brother just ran for his life. He was only 16.

The wailing joined by the Zalgouta* got louder and louder, as his coffin was carried by his young friends, and people threw flowers at his coffin from the windows through the alley as they reached the church. The scout band of drums and brass echoed their pain.

My dad was the Cathedral priest. I asked him once: 'How can you be in a funeral then in a wedding or christening on the same day?' He said for the first year after my oldest brother died, he used to cry at every funeral and then go back to attend the grief of others, his calling was to comfort. My adult voice tells me that he grieved for his child for much longer than a year, more like a lifetime, silently, as did my mum.

I suppose life was not too mean, my parents had more children, us, who lived and survived during their lifetime. I like to think that we brought pleasure to their lives, at least while we were small!

*A Zalgouta is best described as the act of ululating, is a form of a long, wavering, high-pitched vocal sound representing trills of joy.

I came from there

I stood in the courtyard, my father went back to his office, mum had just slipped away to call her sister, my siblings were chatting to each other. The discussion just came to an end. They all left. I stood there alone. No one to talk to.
The world outside was marvellous, full of the pull of the unknown
I opened the main door and left.
I climbed back to the terrace, stood there silent watching them.
I was away miles away, yet they were as close as if I'd never left
I came from there, from the silence of watching.

I lived in

In that old city I walked on a Roman road, I went under Roman arches on my way. I lived in a place rich beyond your imagination. I watched, savoured, stored, and filled my heart, my soul, my eyes; the fresh smell of wild greens, the scent of herbs spread by women from villages nearby. I could listen to the sound of living.

Listening to the early call for prayer praising God from the mosque, the Cathedral bell pulled down with such strength its sounds travelled above all the houses. The calls of passing sellers of fruit and veg were a music and song of their own. On winter nights their voices become softer, selling boiled beetroot or boiled corn. The seasons and the religious celebrations were a way to shadow the sadness of a fragile new country and a generation facing the new order of the world, a world they have to live in and adapt to its changes.

What's left from a long time ago?

Warmth brushed with delicate sorrow.

A richness left me never feeling poor.

THE ARRIVAL

What brought you here?

There was a connection between him and me that stepped over the barrier of languages and escaped the culture lenses.

That connection was more than enough to take that rocky trip to a new land, language and new horizon of time that seemed to stretch forever.

Come into my garden' he said.
I blushed with joy. I did not see the blocked gate.
I remember his words, his heartbeat, and his false tooth,
I remember losing the tools to repair an emptiness that started to spread,
Trying to warm what was left of a dream in a frozen space.
As the quagmire swallowed me bit by bit.
My screaming got louder, and his deafness reached its peak.
I grew slowly into an ugly poisoned weed.
I ballooned as a floating corpse in a neglected lake.
Death harvested the remains of loves flakes.

I left my tears and memories in a shoe box on the
shelf.
then crawled back to the gate.
Then I left.

I climb to my house

As I put my right foot on the drive a flame leaps
under it as though the gravel were hot charcoal. I
stop, holding my left foot on the pavement, then lift it
until it rests on the drive.

Now my feet are on the drive. The connection is cut
with the world. It is time, how many times have I
said it! I am climbing the drive of my house. I call it
home; he calls it bricks and mortar. Each step carries
the weight of sadness that has filled my veins over the
years. Every step carries fear. He is in, I check the
time. 6 o'clock.

My hands rummage into my pockets looking for the
door key. I see his shadow behind the double-glazing
door. Shall I ring the bell? He moved further and
disappeared. No mark was left. It is as if he was never

there. I bang on the door with my fist. Not the first time. I gasp for air as though standing in a vacuum.

I am in. We sit at the table. I light a candle. It's time to talk. Words jumble like popcorn inside me. I utter a few. The silence is a bird spreading its wings to protect the nest I built. I lift my eyes to his. The bird flies away. The ceiling descends closer.

There sits a child, playing with the candle flame unaware of my arteries bleeding. My words were ashes. My tears were a spill of milk. My body disconnects as the candlelight shivers. He blows it for fun. Darkness eats me, bit by bit. I gather what is left, pull out from the wreckage of rotten days. Light shoots from my eyes.
 'I'm done.'

The child

It is time, all the signs pointed to it. They had come much earlier than I thought.
It was time!

It was time to induce her. I was handed a living bundle of love. As she settled between my arms I was shaking, not knowing why. Was it joy, fear, or the shock of producing a living being out of my womb. *What am I going to do now she is here?* That is not a project to create or handle, I thought, it's not a trip or a mission but a bundle of love breathing in a different way, a creature that has just landed.

Everything melted away as I sat in a world of tranquillity, I would hold her quietly, feeding her. Anxious was not a word I knew; therefore, I never acknowledged it. The word anxious is a very significant adjective in my life. I was born anxious, lived as an anxious person, married an anxious man, and fed my little girl anxiety with her milk. The moments of calm and quietness were there for long periods, interrupted by anxiousness. It was the outside world that brought that anxiety to the surface. Anxiety I did not even know I felt.

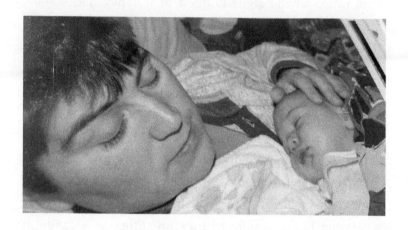

All the signs of labour were there
And the panic to get there, too.
In the zero moment,
dragged by the tiredness of long waiting,
she slides through a slimy noise into light.
Love did not have to rush,
Its seeds had a long time to grow,
To grow into eternal spring.
still, after all these years, my child
still growing and blossoming, my love for you.

54

It was a learning journey to love her without allowing the shade of my protection to stop the brightness of the world outside reaching her, without exposing her early to hard challenges and failure.

Georgette
Her smile is a spring flower.
Her sadness a shy rose bud,
her tears, pearls
Her fresh laugh brightens the night.

What is your name?

Najiba according to my Syrian passport,
Taj tuj according to my brother Habib, the loved one,
Mama according to my mum.
Najoube according to the family...
Gigi according to Ayman

I was called Najiba after my maternal grandmother, a
kind gesture of my father towards his mother-in-law.
Najiba was considered a very old-fashioned name so
there are not many Najibas around! It does make me
special! An Afghani shop keeper pronounces my name
in such a beautiful way. It is a popular name in
Afghanistan. I smile when he says my name and he
smiles at me because I remind him of home and his
cousin.

Taj-touj only my brother Habib calls me, no one else,
he was much younger than me but taller. He would
put his hand on my head, smile and say: *Tuj tuj.*
He departed early, too early, troubled by this world.

'Mama' was my mother's name for me, my sisters, and my brother, later I also called my daughter 'Mama'. Gina the child minder said:
'She will think her name is 'mama'!'
'No, you don't understand! When I call her mama, I mean the love of mama, the heart of mama, the life of mama and the liver of mama. Yes, the liver, the organ that cleanses you. In a way our children cleanse us with their infant purity, with their raw and vital need for us, with their light that touches the sacred.

Gigi is a name that takes me back to a trekking trip in the mountains of Lebanon with Father Paul and forty-nine of us. The name Gigi brings memories of sun, fresh air, and the sound of our voices walking in a long narrow line uphill singing. One line sung by the leader then echoed by us, following, trusting ourselves, trusting the solidity of the ground, the lightness of the air, the beauty that reveals itself as we pushed through the branches with our backpacks, unaware that beneath the green bushes lay a deep drop that would take you to the river. We sang:
in the mountains.... the strong mountains... we hear the air .... we see the sky...we don't touch but the sun .... we will never.... stop climbing

في الجبال.. ذات البأس نسمع الهواء ونرى السماء .لا نلمس الا
الشمس... .. لن نكف عن الصعود

There, in my youth, my connection to beauty
blossomed. It was also a time of discovery. I had
always thought: 'Poverty is having less' but I found
out that the deprivation was much worse when
working with children on the outskirts of the city and
its privileges. Here was a kind of injustice that needed
more than prayers and charitable work. It has pained
me ever since.

More and more names keep sprouting from Najiba:
Naj, Sheeba, Najib, Nashiba. All of them are precious
to me. They were and are voiced by precious people
and born from a long life of memories. Names rightly
or wrongly pronounced can be an opening for a
connection.

***

My lovely neighbour's carer opened the door,
'Pat, Nabija is here!'
I without missing a beat, would reply,
'Hello Ballerie, how are you?'

Where are you from?

'So where are you from?
'I am from Syria
'Come say hello to ……. she is from Saudi.'

That was an afternoon at a house in the outskirts of
Galway in Ireland. It was not a necessity to know
where my country was. I was the one coming to their
country to live as the young wife to an Irishman who
worked in the Middle East. During the thirty years
that followed that afternoon, the answer to 'where is
Syria?' changed every few years.

'Have you heard of Cyprus? Not far from it'
 'Have you heard in the news about Israel's attack on
Lebanon?' Next door to it.
 'You know about the invasion of Iraq? Next door to
it.'
'Gaza, the West Bank, Israel? next door to it.'

Until one day everyone knew where Syria was!

'Are you a refugee? Do you have family there? Aren't
you lucky you live here?'

It is said in good faith. 'war' happens in one of their computer games, films or the pictures of horror published either in the media or by a charity. It remains for a while in the mind then disappears. War is not a game, ask Ester, the delightful friend Ester told me:

'My dear, I looked after my father when he came back from the Great War, and I married a second world war pilot. I know what your people are going through'

Yes, she does, and I believe her in all my heart. The state of alert my mum lived in when I was a child, during and after a war, anxious about getting the basic food, scared for Edward, our neighbour's 18 year, old who had to join the national service as the war erupted, living in dread of the loss of young lives, knowing that the 'enemy' is powerful, and supported by the superpower of the world.

So, I went from being from an unknown place to being from a country defined by its refugees and its extremists, ISL. I moved to Ireland by choice. I was happy building a home, and sank into this new culture without trace, but the core of my being is from the Levant with its sacred alleys and the childhood temple, and it is bleeding slowly with pain and anguish.

But *where are you from?* could sometimes be a way to connect to people who knew the Levant, who were curious, the ones who mentioned the old civilisation, the ones who mentioned the delicious food and the generous ones who praised the kindness of the people.

Where am I from? It is obvious from my strong accent and embarrassing grammatical mistakes that English is not my first language. People are very wary of offending or perhaps they are afraid to voice their curiosity, where *are you from?* The question became a taboo question.

The fear of offending is the offending itself. It is the way to disconnect easily from another person for the sake of keeping things safe. Offend me but talk to me, acknowledge me, we share the same planet after all!

***

'Where are you from?' inquiries

30 years ago, a gentleman in his seventies asked me:
'Where are you from?'
'I am from Syria'
'I visited Damascus, I was in the British Army in
Palestine.' He said Palestine because it was called
*Palestine. ***

> ** In 1917, the British Balfour Declaration*
> *promised the establishment of a Jewish*
> *national home in Ottoman-controlled*
> *Palestine. Britain was granted a Mandate*
> *for Palestine on 25 April 1920.*

***

'Where are you from?'
'I am from Syria?
'Sicily? He smiled, and recited his Italian words very
fast and smiled, looking for an answer. As I was
about to repeat 'Syria', I noticed the long queue in
the library behind him and his wife holding the books
ready to dump them on the counter.
I enlarged my smile, softened my voice, and said:

'Ooooooh,' took the books then said:
'Next!"

***

Another library visitor, they are called customers now,
was a fascinating man who exclaimed: 'Syria? I have
never met anybody from Syria!
This time there was no queue, so I smiled, spun
myself around and said
'Here you are! What do you think?'
Well, it worked. He kept smiling every time he came
to the library, and I smiled too. We each learned
something about the other. We both have an extra
face to smile at, and that is marvellous.

Where is home?

I came with open arms, ready to embrace.

I fell in love with Galway's green land, its ocean. At
Christmas, in Galway Cathedral, listening to one of the
carols 'Silent Night', the one my mum used to sing to
us on Christmas eve. It made me cry. It is then I felt I

was in a foreign land, the people around me were foreign to me. I was a person with no history. A person unknown. If I told a story I had to explain the background in detail till the picture was clear then the story could be told in its historic, and cultural context. If it was a funny story, it was not worth stating the joke.

Having a child changed everything. My daughter was growing, collecting friends, stories, places, collecting joy. I was too, making connections to places through people. I would say.
'This is Suzanne, my first best friend, Sarah is my friend from yoga, Kevin is my colleague: I signed his birthday card'.

Over 30 years I did this so many times the place became familiar and almost a home.

What happened to my birthplace?
The shining jewel that contained all my stories as a little girl in the old city of Damascus.
The narrow alleys, the nearly falling houses, the richness that fills all the senses I saved as a holy place, but only in a moment of severe loneliness could I find comfort to be there. I would stay as long as my

longing lasted then leave, urged on by pain. The two homes extend to reach each other. A blossom tree in a garden in Bristol gives me from the joy I had when I was child under an apricot tree, watching the blossom falling gently in Ghouta.

A frequent question I am asked.
'Do you know which is your home now?'
'Define home for me, what is home for you?'
How can I go back to a childhood place and find it intact as I left it?

I miss the old city. it is still there as it was before me.

I miss that ripple which travels without hesitation till it reaches my gut and my heart

***

That habitual activity, like travelling frequently, that makes the ticket officer smile: 'we have not seen you for a while'
That is also part of home

SO,

We burst from the earth womb to the severity of a life scattered on this wide and limited earth.
Our experiences, our learning and our living widen our vision. With time we don't change, we just see better. The dream is cohesion with the world.

THE AFTER

The years

Years with so many leaves and seasons.
A journey swollen by friends and still.
The child that I bore, baptised in rose water and
musk.
The sweet illusion of falling in love again and again
The strength to face darkness with light.

The empty nest

It starts with their imprints appearing everywhere from the bottom of the laundry basket to their favourite spot on the sofa. Somehow those impressions start to fade and follow them wherever they go next, oblivious to what they pull behind them as they leave. It is that stray woollen thread unravelling from a jumper. The further they move the less that is left of that baby jumper and even less of them to hold.

The pain creeps in like a weed prying apart your closeness and as sharp as a butcher's knife. It slices through you leaving only emptiness behind. Filling that emptiness degrades it in the rush to make it smaller, to repaint it. It does not work. It is still there.

It is a matter of time, they say. They will come back as adults; friends, young parents, giant personalities with a baby's fear and sorrow when things turn sour as it must from time to time.

But now, not yesterday's bag of memories nor tomorrow brimming with hope.

Now, tears pour out like an arterial bleed. Other times it is just a drop, reticent, like a drop of rain granted to a lost soul in a desert.

THE ENCOUNTER

Sue, Rose, and Vicky

Sue

Everybody's name is Sue or another version of Sue.
"I prefer dogs over children," she said.
Everyone raised their eyebrows high behind her back.
Once her pain bled through and showed the marks of
a barren womb and an ancient violent partnership.

Rose

There was something unsaid, untold, reserved with
care from the light. She dropped it by chance in our
last ever encounter. A few details about her past
dysfunction that she bears silently, the open wound
from her crown of thorns that redeems her from her
sins.

Vicky

She, in this frail frame, uncombed hair, mismatched
clothes, neglected nails. She turned and smiled. What
a beautiful girl! She beamed with joy when Van the
man sang. She held within her tight chest the history
of music, beneath her funny skeleton rested the

thousands of books she'd read. Her spidery fingers
bore silver jewellery full of stories about Scottish
kings. If the wind swirled, she could fly and nest in a
tree nearby.

Time, pennies and love she could spare, watering the
earthly needs of a young niece, easing the darkness
and the brain tricks that nested in her sister's world.
We laughed last time we worked together. Her jaw
dropped down and revealed a lioness in her prime.

Gwyneth, Marilyn, Joan, and Lyn

Gwyneth

At the pantomime
Gwyneth put on a costume and danced,
served tea, collected rose petals,
pollen and seeds, in a pocket of air,
'Till, on tiptoe, on an April breeze, she floated up and
away-
She drew out a boat from the shore and sailed...

Marilyn

Marilyn knitted a story bag.
Once she bled a barren womb tale
wailing with pain
On an early August flight,
joy swept her away.

Joan

Joan loved once,
he went to war,
stayed young
like their scribble on a tree.
Her curtains blew like autumn leaves
from the valley of her dreams.
On the first September,
She rose, spread her wings
Then flew away.

Lynn

The morning mist led Lynn away.
her garden, bathed in light, was calling.
She lay, immaculate, awaiting the crossing,
under the bridge, crystallised by frost.

THE DEPARTURE

In Spring

'Let's celebrate her life' they said.
Her pictures - a flowering season of colours — bloomed
in the empty Community hall,   clearing our tears.

In Summer

Her husband left her a space next to him,
lifts his glass 'To my loving wife'
All of us cheered while his voice disappeared
In a whisper that buried her name.

In Autumn

'Let us pray' the priest murmured in a deep voice.
We dropped to our knees and prayed.

In Winter

Her husband offered tea,
Said: 'thank you for coming,'
grabbed death by the neck and left.

LETTERS

A letter to my child

Another year has passed. Another celebration of life's
pulse running through your veins. You stepped into
the woman's fertile land while I was packing to leave.
Your path takes you towards the place where dreams
are renewed, where joy outweighs sorrow. Mine takes
me towards the sunset, to reflect, to hold less
momentum, to seek the smoothness of a sorrow that
nests deep and breathes inner peace.

تبتسم مثل ازهار الربيع
وتحزن بخجل برعم الزهر
وحين تبكي تحضن لؤلؤ دموعها في عينيها الجميلتين
حين تضحك يضحك العالم لها وينتعش الجو ويلمع الليل

A letter to Bet and Bill

My dear Bet and Bill
That evening I met you both was magical. Chance
brought me to that hotel that night. I wonder how
many coincidences brought such a happy time. This
year I will be 60 years old and probably I was born
the month you both met. I suppose paths emerge on
our way and with our inner eyes of the time we
choose the one we think is right. I was occupied for a
very long time with reaching destinations, busy getting
over obstacles to get to a safe shore. Nowadays, I
enjoy the journey more. Take care. Najiba

Dear Najiba
Thank you very much for getting in touch. It would
be good to keep in contact. We'd be delighted to
welcome you to our home.
We had a wonderful trip. After we met you we left to
visit the Church in which we had been married, the
Inn where we had our reception – including the room
in which I'd made my bridegroom's speech 'My wife
and I....' cue loud and raucous applause, and then on
to Cornwall and Devon with the centre-piece a stay

at Lavender Cottage in the Place Manor estate where we spent our first holiday together in the summer of 1956. Incidentally you would not have guessed it meeting Bet and I don't think I told you, but she has Alzheimer's. We combat it, particularly the memory loss aspect, by talking frequently about all sorts of things which have happened in our lives but mostly about the nine months together at university after we first met – it was such a magical time. We do hope you'll find the time to visit us.

With fond good wishes from Bet and me,

Bill

A letter to the man with glasses and moustache

Dear sir,

Don't discard my letter, have a seat, wait a bit.
I saw myself as an alien creature: my top half a bird
and the bottom half stuck in mud, half human, rising
from earth. My laughter and my dreaming lived in
bird's wings. My shame, my shape, my dysfunctional
being, subservient to ready-made rules sank in the
other half. Eagle eyes followed me as my childhood
God spoke; 'you can't hide I am watching you'. I've
only tamed these watching eyes through years. The
outspoken and the shy, the free and the oppressed, the
brightness and the darkness of soul have lived
alongside each other in me.

You walked naked to the sea and swam, then walked
back to the rock. It was beautiful to see a naked body
merging with the water then rising from it.

The following morning early, I walked into the sea,
naked, anxious, bit by bit. I immersed in the delicate
sheet of silver then green of the hill's reflection, then
slid softly away.

Let the breezes scan my cells. Let the water be the green of hills. I dreamed of dance, and I danced in the cracks of changing times and seasons. I dreamed of flying and so I flew, dissolving into the sky that lay in the water around me, mated with my ripples, wrapped around my river of thirst, my tears of delicate longing.

Thank you for dancing your way to the sea on that clear morning on a Mediterranean beach that year.

To Sue, my therapist

As I sat to write a thank-you letter showing my gratitude I heard your voice saying: "it is you who has done the work Najiba". Yes, you are right, it was. It was damned hard and painful work, as much as living.
But you see, you were there,
guiding me, opening spaces,
putting thoughts on the carpet for me to examine if I wished,
Holding my shattered soul in your empathy and silence.
Your core humanity floated as a mirror through which I stared at my darkest moments.
I poured out enough tears to drown your garden.
I poured out enough pain to soften your stone walls.
I scattered a million words to fill your space.
Your kindness was as soft as the flowers in your vase.
As strong as your stone walls were too. Your determination to leave your door all the way open in that space of time called a session.
I, so fragile and haunted by the past, trying to build trust from dust bit by bit. I had to redefine the basis of my being. I shivered naked stripped of every shred

of dignity, covering my shame with a giant fig leaf of
survival skills.
My solitude, the only treasure left in me, I kept
digging deeper to bury.
Dad once asked me why I don't value myself, well,
dad: *I Do Now*!

Mum, I knew, had a desire to be free but duties,
customs and her love for her children chained her.
Well, mum, I too got in that cycle, but I am free,
finally. Free from fear, from guilt, from shame.
So, dear Sue,
I, Najiba, one of many of your therapy's troubled
children, I can face life now. I bow and thank you for
that.

THE LOCKING IN

The call

The cough persisted as I was listening

- I know you are not well but you need to know that from tomorrow teaching will be online ...

The cough persisted as I listened, standing still in the back room staring at the_fir_tree in the next door garden. Its green shades are moving in a harmony like a flock of birds caressing each other. I start following movement of the branches, up and down, in and out. I swing with it. It is too huge to hold my gaze.

Breathe. breathe. it is there for you. it is not going anywhere. It demands nothing from you. Breathe again, the tree is breathing too as a breeze sneaks in a bit. We, the two of us, are breathing. We, the two of us, are bloody stuck here!

The connector

It was a fine day. I stepped out with one foot then the other foot. I closed the door, put the key in my pocket. One step, two steps and then more. The pavement of the street stayed firm under my shaky feet. The trees were washed by light. Too many birds singing. I listened and ease started to spread through my being. The street kept unfolding. For a moment I felt I was losing my balance. People started spinning as though in a race, jumping to the middle of the road, following the guidelines, 2 metres separation.

As for me, in order to hold my balance, I slide away softly keeping them in my gaze as much as I can.

The living

I opened the window. 'Good morning' I said to a bird passing by. Nothing moving, no children in the back gardens, no adults pottering about nearby. In the distance a couple were doing weights in the garden. I rested my eyes there. He passes her a weight; she passes him a towel. I closed my eyes and thought:

`` *you gave someone your glance once as their eyes touched your soft skin'.*

How powerful it is to pass a towel to someone next to you at this moment!

Their connection, in a way, is your joy.

At this moment, they are alive, so I am alive.

I thought that my survival tools in this confined space would help but it did not, only a connection to the living would do.

In the dark nights were my heart rests

Je crois entendre encore,sous les palmiers, Sa voix tendre et sonore Comme un chant de ramiers. Charmant souvenir ! 'Les pêcheurs de perles'

I met Nabil, I must have been 16. I wore the bracelet he gave me day and night. We studied for baccalaureate exams at his house. He offered me the desk near the window. Between our desks a wide-open door filled with his mother's presence, bringing cool drinks or his younger brother running through. He did not say a word. He just smiled when he looked at me. A beautiful smile.

Years rolled on one after another then on a busy day I met a man called Andrew. He kissed me hungrily, freely, deliciously, till my inner voice screamed. I was like the ripples on water, I rippled, every cell rippled till it reached my brain cells one by one, I collapsed into that deep soft cloud, sinking with no ending, wrapped in his arms I fell asleep then woke up as a rose that had just blossomed. That blossom never withered.

Nabil smiling at me, Andrew's looking away became my refuge. I wish I could see them, once more, hold their hands and kiss their eyes.

The weather is changing. It is going to rain, another reason to sit in the dark and cry for a while.

I AM

I am...

I am a bull when I am angry
A butterfly when kind,
A joy when I smile,
A flood when I cry,
A complex machine when I think,
A soft feather pillow when I hug,
A vast valley when I listen,
A deep gorge when I hold other's fears,
And a blue ocean when I am in love.

My joy,

a wave of warmth

nesting in humming a bird's song.

You are not old, they said.

Is it the time to depart from the plane?   The journey?
Life itself?

I am reaching towards a life that has started slipping
from my fingers.

The signs are clear: the shape of the face, the colour
of the skin, the disproportions of physique, short naps
in the day.

It is also there in the increasing fear, the worry that
the overloaded shelves of memory could collapse, the
fear for the heart weakened by pain and living, fear of
the self-destruction of the body itself, consumed by
cancerous cells.

Now it is comforting, slowing down to see more,
savouring a lot from a very little, embracing beauty in
its microscopic details.

I need a daily dose of love to flourish

Daily Exercise

Hold my delicate heart,
release the birds of thoughts to feed the soul,
caress the pain of ageing body,
walk smoothly without disturbing
the sheet of air,
the stillness of light.

Love did not have to rush,
Its seeds had a long time to grow,
To grow into eternal spring.

THANKS,

To every kind soul who whispered a word, held my hands, hugged me, made me soup, shared their joy with me.

Acknowledgement

The intuitive writing craft seminar by Joseph Williams brought my work into the light.
www.intuitivewritingcraft.com

Layout and typesetting by Anthony Lane.
anthonylane13@protonmail.com

Special thanks to:

Malak Mouracade
Allegra and Peter Stone
Anoir Ou-Chad
Belinda Rimmer
Caroline Jones
Colette Campbell
Heather Nadir-Jones
Isobel McKenzie - Price
John Mc Lellan
Liggy Webb
www.liggywebb.com